EAST AFRICA TRAVEL GUIDE 2026

Kenya • Tanzania • Uganda • Rwanda • Zanzibar

By **Adrian Luca**

DISCLAIMER

This book is intended for **informational and travel guidance purposes only**. While every effort has been made to ensure the accuracy, reliability, and completeness of the information provided, **travel conditions, prices, regulations, and requirements may change at any time**. Readers are encouraged to verify details such as visas, transportation, entry rules, health guidelines, and safety information with official government sources, local authorities, or professional travel services before making travel decisions.

The author, Adrian Luca, and the publisher are **not responsible for any loss, injury, inconvenience, or damages** that may occur as a result of using the information contained in this book.
All travel is done at the reader's own risk and responsibility.

Any opinions expressed in this guide are based on the author's research, knowledge, and experience at the time of writing.

All trademarks, names, locations, and brands mentioned in this book remain the property of their respective owners and are used only for descriptive and informational purposes.

© **2025Adrian Luca**

All Rights Reserved.

No part of this book may be reproduced, stored, or transmitted without written permission from the publisher, except in the case of brief quotations.

Published by:Adrian Luca**Travel Books**

FULL BOOK DESCRIPTION
CHAPTER 1 — Welcome to East Africa

- Overview of the region
- What makes East Africa magical
- How to plan the perfect 2026 adventure
- Best time to visit each country
- Budget ranges (budget / mid / luxury)

CHAPTER 2 — Essential Travel Information for 2026

- Visa requirements for each country
- New 2026 entry rules
- Vaccination & health requirements
- Money, SIM cards & safety
- Cultural etiquette (very important for East Africa)

CHAPTER 3 — Kenya: Land of the Great Migration

Must-Visit Places

- Maasai Mara
- Amboseli

- Tsavo East & West
- Diani Beach
- Nairobi National Park

Hidden Gems

- Samburu
- Kakamega Forest
- Lamu Island

Local culture

What to eat

7-day Kenya itinerary

CHAPTER 4 — Tanzania: Home of the Serengeti & Kilimanjaro

Must-Visit Places

- Serengeti
- Ngorongoro Crater
- Mount Kilimanjaro
- Tarangire
- Lake Manyara

Beaches

- Dar es Salaam
- Bagamoyo

Hidden Gems

- Udzungwa Mountains
- Mafia Island

Culture & cuisine

Tanzania 2026 travel costs

7-day & 10-day itineraries

CHAPTER 5 — Zanzibar: The Pearl of the Indian Ocean

Top Beaches

- Nungwi
- Kendwa
- Paje
- Michamvi

Attractions

- Stone Town

- Spice Farms
- Prison Island

Hidden Islands

- Mnemba
- Chumbe

Best resorts (budget–luxury)

Honeymoon & family activities

CHAPTER 6 — Uganda: Gorillas, Waterfalls & Adventure

Must-Visit Places

- Bwindi Impenetrable Forest
- Murchison Falls
- Queen Elizabeth Park
- Jinja (source of the Nile)

Hidden Gems

- Sipi Falls
- Lake Bunyonyi

Local culture

Gorilla permit costs (2026 updates)

Travel routes & itineraries

CHAPTER 7 — Rwanda: Clean, Safe & Culturally Rich

Must-Visit Places

- Volcanoes National Park
- Kigali
- Nyungwe Forest
- Lake Kivu

Culture, cleanliness & safety

How to do gorilla trekking in Rwanda

5-day & 7-day itineraries

CHAPTER 8 — Multi-Country Itineraries

- Kenya + Tanzania Safari
- Kenya + Uganda (Gorilla Trekking)
- Tanzania + Zanzibar

- 14-Day East Africa Master Itinerary
- 21-Day Grand East Africa Loop

CHAPTER 9 — Budgeting & Money-Saving Secrets

- Cheapest safari options
- Budget-friendly beaches
- Avoiding tourist scams
- Transport tips
- When to book for the best prices

CHAPTER 10 — Accommodation Guide

- Best budget, mid-range & luxury stays per country
- Tented camps
- Lodge recommendations
- City hotels
- Beach resorts

CHAPTER 11 — Packing List for 2026

- Safari clothes
- Beach essentials

- Drone rules
- Gadgets
- Travel health kit

CHAPTER 12 — Cultural Respect & Local Customs

- Respectful greetings
- What NOT to do
- Dress codes
- Tipping etiquette
- Photography etiquette
- How to connect with locals warmly

CHAPTER 13 — Hidden Gems Across East Africa

- Secret waterfalls
- Undiscovered islands
- Local food markets
- Cultural villages
- Off-the-path safari camps

CHAPTER 14 — Safety, Transport & Practical Tips

- Safety do's and don'ts

- Best local airlines
- Bus/boat/train options
- Border crossing rules
- 2026 updates

CHAPTER 1 Welcome to East Africa

Overview of the Region

East Africa is one of the most breathtaking travel regions on Earth, stretching from the golden plains of **Kenya** to the volcanic mountains of **Tanzania**, the emerald rainforests of **Uganda**, the rolling hills of **Rwanda**, and the turquoise beaches of **Zanzibar**. It is a region defined by:

- The world's greatest wildlife migrations
- Iconic national parks and UNESCO wonders
- Warm, welcoming cultures

- **A blend of modern cities and untouched natural beauty**

Whether you're chasing wildlife, beaches, culture, food, adventure, or relaxation, East Africa offers an unforgettable experience for every traveler.

What Makes East Africa Magical

East Africa is magical because of its **diversity and authenticity**. Here's why travelers fall in love instantly:

1. Legendary Wildlife Safaris

Home to the **Big Five**—lion, elephant, buffalo, rhino, leopard—East Africa hosts the world-famous **Great Migration**, where millions of wildebeest and zebras cross the Serengeti–Mara ecosystem.

2. Dream Beaches & Tropical Islands

Zanzibar's white sands, crystal-clear waters, coral reefs, and ancient Arabic architecture make it a paradise for beach lovers.

3. High Mountains & Volcanoes

Mount Kilimanjaro, Africa's highest peak, attracts climbers from around the world.

Rwanda and Uganda offer rare encounters with **mountain gorillas** in misty volcano forests.

4. Culture, Food & Warm Hospitality

From Maasai traditions to Swahili cuisine, East Africa blends history, spices, music, and colorful markets in a way no other region does.

5. Adventure Everywhere

Safaris, hot-air balloons, mountain trekking, snorkeling, diving, gorilla trekking, cultural tours, night markets — the region is packed with excitement.

How to Plan the Perfect 2026 Adventure

Planning your East Africa trip becomes easier with the right order and preparation.

1. Choose Your Main Purpose

- Safari
- Beach holiday
- Gorilla trekking
- Cultural exploration
- Adventure activities

- A combination of everything

2. Select Countries Based on Your Goal

- **Kenya** → wildlife safaris, Nairobi city life, Maasai Mara
- **Tanzania** → Serengeti, Kilimanjaro, Zanzibar beaches
- **Uganda** → gorillas, lakes, forests
- **Rwanda** → luxury gorilla trekking, Kigali city
- **Zanzibar** → beaches, spice tours, relaxation

3. Plan Your Budget Level

(See "Budget ranges" section below)

4. Arrange Documents

- Passport valid for **6+ months**
- E-visa (online for Kenya, Uganda, Rwanda, Tanzania)
- Yellow Fever certificate (often required)

5. Build a 7–14 Day Itinerary

Examples:

- **Kenya + Tanzania (10 days)** — best for wildlife lovers

- **Uganda + Rwanda (7–9 days)** — best for gorillas and nature
- **Zanzibar (5–7 days)** — perfect for beaches and relaxation

6. Book Early for 2026

2026 is expected to be a high-travel year, especially during Great Migration season — make reservations early.

Best Time to Visit Each Country

KENYA

- Best: **July–October** (Migration), **January–February**
- Avoid: April–May (long rains)

TANZANIA

- Best: **June–October**
- Zanzibar best months: **June–February**

UGANDA

- Best: **June–September**, **December–February** (trekking seasons)

RWANDA

- Best: **June–September, December–January**

ZANZIBAR

- Best: **June–October, December–February**
- Avoid: April (heavy rain)

Budget Ranges (Budget / Mid Luxury)

1. Budget Travel

- **$40–$80 per day**
- Hostels/guesthouses
- Group safaris
- Local food stalls
- Public transport & shared vehicles

2. Mid-Range Travel

- **$120–$250 per day**
- Boutique hotels & mid-range lodges
- Private safaris
- Domestic flights available
- Beach resorts in Zanzibar

3. Luxury Travel

- **$350–$1500+ per day**
- High-end lodges (Serengeti, Mara, Volcanoes NP)
- Hot-air balloons
- Private guides & exclusive 4x4 vehicles
- 5-star beachfront resorts

CHAPTER 2 — Essential Travel Information for 2026

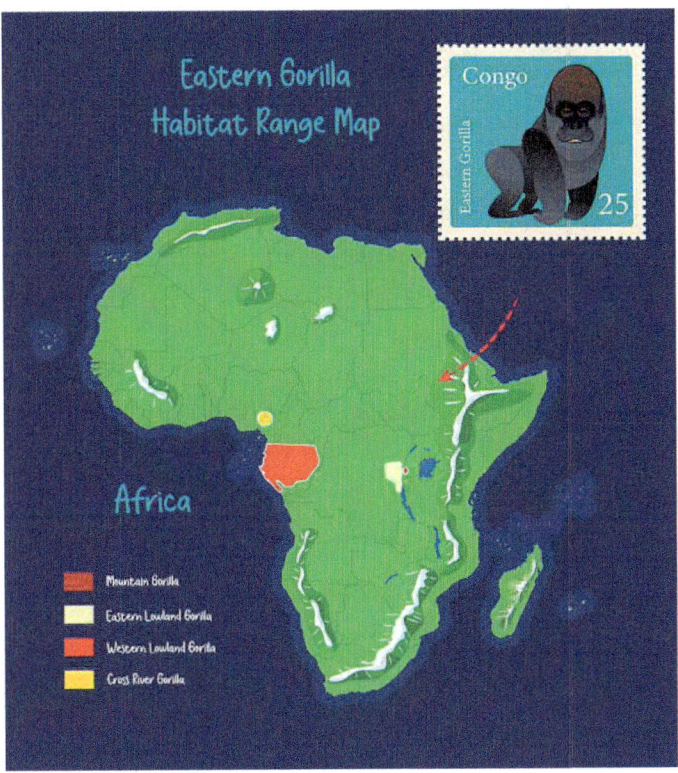

Traveling through East Africa in 2026 is easier, safer, and smoother than ever. This chapter gives you everything you must know before arriving — visas, entry rules, health requirements, money, SIM cards, etiquette, and more.

Visa Requirements for Each Country (2026)

🏳 Kenya

- Kenya now uses the **Electronic Travel Authorization (eTA)** system.
- Apply online before arrival.
- Most travelers get approval within **72 hours**.

🏳 Tanzania

- Tanzania offers an **eVisa** for most nationalities.
- Approval normally takes **3–7 days**.
- Visa on arrival exists, but **eVisa is recommended**.

🏳 Uganda

- Uganda uses a full **online eVisa** system.
- The **East Africa Tourist Visa** is also available and extremely popular.

🏳 Rwanda

- Rwanda offers **visa on arrival** for almost all travelers.

- For safari and multi-country trips, the **East Africa Tourist Visa** is the best choice.

🏳 Zanzibar (Part of Tanzania)

- Same visa rules as Tanzania.
- Visitors arriving directly to Zanzibar must also show **eVisa confirmation**.

The East Africa Tourist Visa (Highly Recommended)

This visa allows travel to **Kenya, Uganda, and Rwanda on one single visa**.

- Valid for **90 days**
- Perfect for combined safari + gorilla trekking trips
- Must be obtained **before arrival**
- Tanzania and Zanzibar not included

New 2026 Entry Rules

East Africa continues to modernize its entry systems.

1. Mandatory Online Travel Pre-Registration

Most countries now require:

- Passport details
- Accommodation information
- Return flight information
- Emergency contact

Submit **before arrival** online.

2. Stricter Health Screening

Airports may require:

- Temperature checks
- Basic health questionnaires
- Proof of certain vaccinations (see below)

3. Biometric Verification

Kenya, Rwanda, and Tanzania use fingerprint or facial recognition at immigration for faster entry.

4. Digital Payments

Many airports and border posts now prefer:

- **Card payments**
- **Mobile payments**
- Less reliance on cash

Vaccination & Health Requirements (2026)

Required / Common Vaccines

- **Yellow Fever** (important for Kenya, Uganda, Rwanda, Tanzania)
- Routine vaccines (MMR, polio, tetanus)

Recommended Vaccines

- Typhoid
- Hepatitis A & B
- Rabies (if doing wildlife or outdoor adventures)

Malaria Prevention

East Africa has malaria zones in many areas. Recommended:

- Mosquito repellent
- Long sleeves at night
- Anti-malarial medication (speak to a doctor)

Travel Insurance

Highly recommended for:

- Medical emergencies

- Lost luggage
- Flight delays
- Safari or adventure injuries

Money, SIM Cards & Safety

Money

Currencies in the region:

- **Kenyan Shilling (KES)**
- **Tanzanian Shilling (TZS)**
- **Ugandan Shilling (UGX)**
- **Rwandan Franc (RWF)**
- **US Dollar (USD)** widely accepted in safaris and hotels.

🔔 **Tip:** Bring new USD notes (issued after 2013). Old notes may be rejected.

SIM Cards (Easy to Get)

- **Kenya:** Safaricom
- **Tanzania/Zanzibar:** Vodacom
- **Uganda:** MTN
- **Rwanda:** MTN Rwanda

Airport SIM counters are cheap:

- $5–$15 for data packages

- Free registration with your passport

Safety (2026)

East Africa is generally safe for travelers if you follow normal precautions:

- Avoid walking late at night in isolated places
- Keep belongings close in busy areas
- Use official taxis or ride apps
- Avoid showing expensive jewelry
- Follow your tour guide's instructions during wildlife activities

Most tourist areas are well-patrolled and secure.

Cultural Etiquette (Very Important in East Africa)

East Africa has warm, respectful cultures. Showing good manners will make your trip smoother and more enjoyable.

1. Greetings Matter

Always greet people first:

- "Habari" (How are you?) — Kenya
- "Jambo" (Hello) — Tanzania

- "Mulembe" / "Oli otya?" — Uganda
- "Muraho" — Rwanda
- "Salaam Alaikum" — Zanzibar coastal areas

2. Dress Respectfully in Rural Areas

Cities are modern, but villages prefer:

- Covered shoulders
- Not-too-short shorts
- No overly revealing outfits

3. Respect Local Customs

- Ask before taking photos of people
- Remove shoes before entering some homes
- Do not touch someone's head (culturally sensitive)

4. Keep Your Voice Calm

East Africa values calm and polite communication.

5. Eating Etiquette

- Use your right hand when eating local meals
- Accept food or drink politely

6. Respect Wildlife

Never:

- Touch wild animals
- Feed them
- Leave your vehicle without permission

7. Tipping Culture

Tipping is appreciated:

- $5–$20 per day for safari guides
- 5–10% at restaurants
- $1 for assistance at hotels or airports

CHAPTER 3 — Kenya: Land of the Great Migration

Kenya is one of Africa's most iconic travel destinations — home of the **Great Wildebeest Migration**, world-famous national parks, spectacular beaches, warm hospitality, and unforgettable cultural encounters. Whether you love wildlife, cities, beaches, or culture, Kenya offers a powerful blend of adventure and beauty.

Must-Visit Places

1. Maasai Mara National Reserve

The jewel of Kenya and one of the **world's greatest safari destinations**.

Highlights:

- The **Great Migration** (July–October)
- Endless savannah plains
- Big Five sightings
- Hot-air balloon safaris
- Maasai cultural villages

Maasai Mara is the heart of East Africa's wildlife and one of the most photographed landscapes on Earth.

2. Amboseli National Park

Known as the **land of elephants** and the **best views of Mount Kilimanjaro**.

Why visitors love it:

- Large elephant herds
- Beautiful sunsets
- Close-range wildlife photography
- Stunning Kilimanjaro backdrop

Amboseli offers one of the most dramatic safari sceneries in Africa.

3. Tsavo East & Tsavo West

These twin parks form one of the **largest conservation areas** in Africa.

Tsavo East: wide open landscapes, red soil, enormous herds of elephants.
  Tsavo West: volcanic formations, natural springs, black rhino sanctuary.

Perfect for travelers who want a wilder, less crowded, more authentic safari experience.

4. Diani Beach

One of the **most beautiful beaches in Africa**, with turquoise waters, palm trees, and white sand.

Activities:

- Snorkeling & diving
- Dhow cruises
- Skydiving
- Camel rides on the beach
- Luxury beachfront resorts

A perfect beach extension after a safari.

5. Nairobi National Park

The only national park on Earth located inside a major capital city.

Why it's special:

- Lions, rhinos, giraffes — with the Nairobi skyline behind them
- Easy half-day or full-day safari
- Close to the airport — great for quick trips

A perfect introduction to Kenya's wildlife.

Hidden Gems

1. Samburu National Reserve

A rugged, semi-desert region filled with unique animals found nowhere else.

Special wildlife (the Samburu Five):

- Grevy's zebra
- Somali ostrich
- Beisa oryx
- Reticulated giraffe
- Gerenuk (the "giraffe antelope")

Home to the Samburu people — known for their beautiful attire and traditions.

2. Kakamega Forest

One of the last remaining tropical rainforests in Kenya.

Why visit:

- Birdwatcher's paradise
- Butterfly species
- Primate encounters
- Magical hiking trails

Perfect for nature lovers seeking peace and green beauty.

3. Lamu Island (UNESCO World Heritage Site)

A tranquil Swahili island with ancient architecture, dhow boats, and peaceful beaches.

Why it's special:

- No cars — donkeys and boats only
- Old Town architecture
- Arabian-African cultural blend
- Sunset dhow cruises

A paradise for travelers who want culture, history, and relaxation.

Local Culture

Kenya is home to over **40 ethnic groups**, each with its own traditions, languages, food, and festivals.

Cultural highlights:

- Maasai and Samburu warrior traditions
- Swahili culture on the coast
- Colorful beadwork and crafts
- Music, dance, and storytelling
- Warm greetings and hospitality

Kenyans value respect, friendliness, and community — travelers always feel welcomed.

What to Eat

Kenyan cuisine is vibrant and delicious.

Top dishes to try:

- **Ugali** — the national dish made from maize flour
- **Nyama Choma** — grilled meat, especially goat or beef
- **Chapati** — soft, flaky bread
- **Pilau** — spiced rice influenced by Swahili cuisine
- **Sukuma Wiki** — sautéed greens

- **Mandazi** — fried coconut dough snacks
- **Fresh seafood** — especially on the coast

Kenya's food is flavorful, warm, and comforting.

7-Day Kenya Itinerary (Perfect for 2026)

Day 1 — Arrive in Nairobi

- Visit Nairobi National Park
- Giraffe Centre
- Karen Blixen Museum
- Dinner at local restaurants

Day 2 — Fly or drive to Maasai Mara

- Afternoon game drive
- Sunset over the savannah

Day 3 — Full-day Safari in Maasai Mara

- Tracking lions, leopards, elephants
- Optional hot-air balloon at sunrise

Day 4 — Return to Nairobi → Amboseli

- Drive to Amboseli
- Evening wildlife viewing

Day 5 — Explore Amboseli

- Elephant herds
- Kilimanjaro viewpoints
- Birdlife photography

Day 6 — Fly to Diani Beach (Mombasa)

- Relax on white sand beaches
- Snorkeling or dhow cruise

Day 7 — Diani Beach → Departure

- Beach morning
- Fly back to Nairobi for international departure

Perfect blend of **wildlife + culture + beach**.

CHAPTER 4 —Tanzania: Home of the Serengeti & Kilimanjaro

Tanzania is one of the most extraordinary travel destinations on Earth — home to the iconic **Serengeti**, the world-famous **Ngorongoro Crater**, the majestic **Mount Kilimanjaro**, and some of Africa's most beautiful beaches and cultural heritage sites.

In 2026, Tanzania remains a top bucket-list destination for safari lovers, adventurers, and beach travelers.

Must-Visit Places

1. Serengeti National Park

One of Earth's most legendary wildlife destinations.

Why it's world-famous:

- Home of the **Great Wildebeest Migration**
- Endless golden plains filled with lions, cheetahs, elephants
- Best safari photography in Africa
- Luxury lodges and mobile camps following the migration

Best time: **June–October** (dry season), **December–February** (calving season).

2. Ngorongoro Crater

Often called **"Africa's Garden of Eden"** — a breathtaking volcanic crater packed with wildlife.

Highlights:

- High chance to see the **Big Five**
- Beautiful landscapes
- Maasai villages around the crater rim
- UNESCO World Heritage Site

One of Africa's most rewarding single-day safaris.

3. Mount Kilimanjaro

The highest mountain in Africa (5,895 m) and the world's tallest free-standing mountain.

Why travelers love it:

- Suitable for beginners with proper preparation
- No technical climbing required
- Seven different trekking routes
- Stunning glacier views

Best months: **January–March** and **July–October**.

4. Tarangire National Park

Famous for its massive elephant herds and beautiful landscapes covered with giant baobab trees.

Highlights:

- Best in dry season (June–October)
- Elephants in huge numbers
- Birdlife paradise
- Quiet and less crowded than Serengeti

Perfect for photographers and nature lovers.

5. Lake Manyara National Park

A small but magical park known for:

- **Tree-climbing lions**
- Flamingos
- Hot springs
- Scenic forests and lakeside views

Ideal for families, first-time safari visitors, and short safaris.

Beaches

Dar es Salaam

A lively coastal city and Tanzania's main port, offering:

- Oceanfront restaurants
- Beaches like Coco Beach
- Access to Zanzibar ferries

Best for travelers who enjoy a mix of city + beach life.

Bagamoyo

A historic Swahili-Arab town with quiet beaches and rich heritage.

Why visit:

- UNESCO World Heritage site (pending)

- Old German colonial buildings
- Scenic waterfront
- Relaxed beaches with fewer tourists

A peaceful alternative to Zanzibar.

Hidden Gems

1. Udzungwa Mountains National Park

A lush rainforest paradise known as the **"African Galápagos"** for its unique species.

Highlights:

- Stunning hiking trails
- Sanje Waterfalls (170 meters)
- Rare primates found nowhere else
- Birdwatching heaven

Perfect for nature lovers seeking off-the-beaten-path adventures.

2. Mafia Island

A quiet tropical island far less crowded than Zanzibar.

Why it's special:

- One of the best diving spots in Africa
- Whale shark sightings (October–March)
- Coral reefs and marine parks
- Pristine beaches perfect for relaxation

Ideal for travelers seeking peace and underwater beauty.

Culture & Cuisine

Culture

Tanzania is home to more than **120 ethnic groups**, creating a colorful mix of traditions.

Cultural highlights:

- Maasai and Hadzabe tribes
- Swahili coastal culture
- Traditional music: *ngoma* drums, taarab
- Warm, polite greetings ("Jambo", "Habari")

Respectful communication and friendliness are important in daily life.

Cuisine

Tanzanian food is flavorful, warm, and influenced by African, Indian, and Swahili traditions.

Top dishes to try:

- **Ugali** — maize porridge, national dish
- **Nyama Choma** — grilled meat
- **Pilau** — spiced Swahili rice
- **Zanzibar biryani** — rich, aromatic rice
- **Mishkaki** — marinated meat skewers
- **Fresh seafood** — especially prawns, lobster, octopus

Coastal cuisine is rich in coconut, spices, and fresh fish.

Tanzania 2026 Travel Costs

Budget Travel

- **$50–$100 per day**
- Budget lodges, group safaris, public transport

Mid-Range Travel

- **$150–$300 per day**
- Mid-range lodges, domestic flights, private safaris

Luxury Travel

- **$400–$1500+ per day**

- Luxury lodges (Serengeti, Ngorongoro)
- Private 4x4 vehicles
- Balloon safaris
- High-end beach resorts

Tanzania is perfect for every type of traveler.

7-Day Tanzania Itinerary (Perfect for Safaris)

Day 1 — Arrive in Arusha

Rest, city tour, local food.

Day 2 — Tarangire National Park

Elephants, baobab trees, birdlife.

Day 3 — Lake Manyara

Tree-climbing lions, flamingos.

Day 4 — Serengeti (Central)

Enter Serengeti, sunset game drive.

Day 5 — Serengeti (Full Day)

Tracking predators, plains wildlife.

Day 6 — Ngorongoro Crater

Big Five, crater views, Maasai villages.

Day 7 — Arusha → Departure

City markets, coffee tours, fly home.

10-Day Tanzania Safari + Kilimanjaro + Beach Itinerary

Days 1–2 — Arusha + Tarangire

Start with classic safari landscapes.

Days 3–4 — Serengeti

Migration, cheetahs, lions.

Days 5–6 — Ngorongoro Crater

Big Five, breathtaking crater scenery.

Days 7–8 — Fly to Zanzibar

Beaches, Stone Town, spice tours.

Days 9–10 — Nungwi / Kendwa

White sand beaches, snorkeling, sunset cruises.

A perfect mix of **wildlife + adventure + beach paradise**.

CHAPTER 5 — Zanzibar: The Pearl of the Indian Ocean

Zanzibar is one of the most magical places in East Africa — a tropical paradise of **white-sand beaches**, **turquoise waters**, **Swahili culture**, and **historic charm**. Known as the **"Spice Island,"** Zanzibar combines culture, beach relaxation, adventure, and world-class resorts.

In 2026, it remains one of Africa's *most visited* beach destinations, perfect for couples, families, and solo travelers.

Top Beaches in Zanzibar (2026)

1. Nungwi Beach

One of the most popular and vibrant beaches on the island.

Why travelers love it:

- Clear turquoise water
- No strong tides — perfect for swimming
- Great nightlife and beach restaurants
- Turtle conservation center
- Snorkeling and dhow cruises

Perfect for young travelers, couples, and anyone who loves a lively beach vibe.

2. Kendwa Beach

Often considered the **best sunset spot** in Zanzibar.

Highlights:

- Calm waters all day
- Wide sandy beaches
- Luxury resorts and beach bars
- Famous Full Moon Party events

Kendwa is ideal for sunset lovers and travelers who want luxury and fun.

3. Paje Beach

A paradise for **adventurers and kite surfers**.

Why it's special:

- Long white-sand beach
- Shallow turquoise lagoon
- One of the world's top kitesurfing locations
- Cool cafés, guesthouses, and hostels

Perfect for young travelers, digital nomads, and water-sport lovers.

4. Michamvi Peninsula

Peaceful, romantic, and more secluded.

Highlights:

- Incredible sunsets
- Quiet beaches
- Tide pools for exploring
- Lovely boutique hotels

Michamvi is perfect for couples and those seeking calm relaxation.

Top Attractions & Experiences

1. Stone Town (UNESCO World Heritage Site)

A cultural treasure filled with history, narrow alleyways, and Swahili-Arab architecture.

Must-see places:

- Old Fort
- House of Wonders
- Forodhani Gardens Night Market
- Darajani Market
- Freddie Mercury House

A perfect mix of culture, food, and history.

2. Spice Farms ("Spice Tours")

Zanzibar is known as the **Spice Island** for a reason.

Learn about:

- Cardamom
- Cloves
- Cinnamon
- Nutmeg
- Vanilla
- Traditional farming
- Local medicine & herbs

A wonderful cultural and culinary experience.

3. Prison Island (Changuu Island)

A small island famous for its giant tortoises.

Highlights:

- Aldabra giant tortoises (some over 100 years old!)
- Snorkeling in clear waters
- Historic quarantine buildings
- Perfect half-day trip

Very popular with families.

Hidden Islands & Secret Spots

1. Mnemba Island

A private island with one of the best marine reserves in East Africa.

Why it's special:

- Crystal-clear water
- Coral reefs
- Dolphins
- Turtle nesting
- Luxury resort

Perfect for snorkeling, diving, and honeymooners.

2. Chumbe Island Marine Sanctuary

A fully protected eco-island.

Highlights:

- Rare coral species
- Eco-friendly bungalows
- Forest walks
- Pristine snorkeling

Great for eco-conscious travelers and nature lovers.

Best Resorts (Budget – Mid – Luxury)

Budget (Affordable but great quality)

- New Teddy's on the Beach (Paje)
- Paje by Night Hotel
- Kendwa Rocks (Kendwa)

Perfect for backpackers and budget travelers.

Mid-Range

- Amaan Beach Bungalows (Nungwi)
- Zuri Zanzibar (stylish & modern)
- Zanzibar Queen Hotel (Matemwe)

Great for families and couples.

Luxury (Top global standards)

- The Residence Zanzibar
- Essque Zalu Zanzibar
- Melia Zanzibar
- Mnemba Island Lodge (ultra-luxury private island)

Perfect for honeymooners and high-end travelers.

Honeymoon Activities

Zanzibar is one of the top **honeymoon destinations in Africa**.

Best romantic experiences:

- Sunset dhow cruises
- Private beach dinners
- Couples' spa treatments
- Sandbank picnics
- Swimming with dolphins (Kizimkazi)
- Luxury resort stays

Perfect for unforgettable romantic moments.

Family Activities

Zanzibar is safe and family-friendly.

Top family experiences:

- Giant tortoises at Prison Island
- Snorkeling trips
- Spice tours
- Butterfly Centre
- Jozani Forest (Red Colobus Monkeys)
- Calm beaches in Kendwa & Nungwi

Families love the nature, culture, and calm atmosphere.

CHAPTER 6 — Uganda: Gorillas, Waterfalls & Adventure

Uganda is one of Africa's most breathtaking destinations — a place of **mountain gorillas**, dramatic **waterfalls**, lush forests, sparkling lakes, and warm, welcoming people. Known as the **"Pearl of Africa,"** Uganda offers a powerful mix of adventure, nature, and culture that is unlike anywhere else in East Africa.

In 2026, Uganda continues to rise as a top bucket-list destination, especially for travelers seeking gorilla trekking, wildlife safaris, and outdoor adventures.

Must-Visit Places

1. Bwindi Impenetrable Forest (Gorilla Trekking Capital)

A UNESCO World Heritage Site and one of the last places on Earth where **mountain gorillas** live.

Why travelers love it:

- Home to nearly half of the world's gorillas
- Once-in-a-lifetime gorilla trekking
- Dense, magical rainforest
- Community villages and local crafts

Trekking takes 2–6 hours depending on gorilla movements, and the experience is unforgettable.

2. Murchison Falls National Park

Home to the **most powerful waterfall in the world**.

Highlights:

- Boat cruise on the Nile
- Game drives with lions, buffalo, elephants
- Hiking to the top of the falls
- Beautiful sunsets on the river

The sight of the Nile squeezing through a narrow 7-meter gap is one of Africa's greatest natural wonders.

3. Queen Elizabeth National Park

A diverse and scenic park famous for:

Attractions:

- Tree-climbing lions in Ishasha
- Kazinga Channel boat cruise
- Hippos, elephants, buffalo
- Crater lakes and volcanic cones
- Chimp trekking in Kyambura Gorge

Perfect for travelers who want a mix of safari, water adventures, and landscapes.

4. Jinja — Source of the Nile

The adventure capital of East Africa.

Top experiences:

- Nile river rafting
- Bungee jumping (age-dependent rules apply)
- Boat rides at the Nile source
- Quad biking and horseback riding
- Beautiful cafes and riverside lodges

A fun and energetic destination, perfect for outdoor lovers and travelers who enjoy river scenery.

Hidden Gems

1. Sipi Falls

A collection of three stunning waterfalls on the slopes of Mount Elgon.

Why visit:

- Breathtaking mountain views
- Coffee farm tours
- Hiking trails for all levels
- Peaceful and cool climate

One of Uganda's most photogenic places.

2. Lake Bunyonyi

Often called **"the Switzerland of Africa"** because of its beautiful terraced hills.

Highlights:

- Canoe rides
- Island tours
- Birds and nature
- Romantic lakeside lodges

- Peaceful swimming areas

Located close to Bwindi, it's the perfect place to relax before or after gorilla trekking.

Local Culture

Uganda is home to more than **50 ethnic groups**, each with unique music, dance, crafts, and traditions.

Cultural highlights:

- Baganda Kingdom culture in Kampala
- Traditional dances like *Bakisimba*
- Markets full of fabrics, crafts, bananas, fruits
- Respectful greetings and friendliness
- Community tourism experiences in villages around Bwindi and Sipi

Ugandans are known for being warm and welcoming to visitors.

Gorilla Permit Costs (2026 Updates)

Gorilla trekking is Uganda's most popular activity.

Uganda Gorilla Permit Price (2026):

- **$700 USD** per person (foreign travelers)

The permit includes:

- Park entry
- Ranger guides
- Gorilla family allocation
- Safety briefing

Best booking time: 3–6 months before travel
Best trekking months: June–September, December–February

Travel Routes & Itineraries

7-Day Uganda Highlights Itinerary

Day 1 — Arrive in Entebbe / Kampala
City tour, craft markets, local food.

Day 2 — Drive to Murchison Falls
Visit the top of the falls.

Day 3 — Murchison Safari + Nile Boat Cruise
Elephants, lions, hippos, crocodiles.

Day 4 — Transfer to Queen Elizabeth Park
Crater lake viewpoints along the way.

Day 5 — Queen Elizabeth Safari + Kazinga Channel
Boat cruise, wildlife viewing.

Day 6 — Drive to Bwindi Impenetrable Forest
Relax in the rainforest.

Day 7 — Gorilla Trekking → Lake Bunyonyi → Departure
One of the world's greatest wildlife experiences.

10-Day Uganda Ultimate Adventure Itinerary

Days 1–2 — Kampala + Jinja
Visit the Nile, boat rides, waterfalls.

Days 3–4 — Murchison Falls
Safari + top-of-the-falls hike.

Days 5–6 — Queen Elizabeth Park
Tree-climbing lions, boat cruises.

Days 7–8 — Bwindi Gorilla Trekking
Meet mountain gorillas in the wild.

Days 9–10 — Lake Bunyonyi
Relax, canoe, explore islands and culture.

A perfect trip for both adventure and relaxation.

CHAPTER 7 — Rwanda: Clean, Safe & Culturally Rich

Rwanda is one of Africa's fastest-rising travel destinations — a country known for its **extraordinary cleanliness**, **world-class safety**, **welcoming culture**, and breathtaking natural landscapes.

Famously called the **"Land of a Thousand Hills,"** Rwanda offers unforgettable experiences such as **gorilla trekking**, peaceful lakeside towns, and one of Africa's most modern capitals.

In 2026, Rwanda stands out as a destination perfect for travelers seeking **luxury, culture, nature, and safety** all in one place.

Must-Visit Places

1. Volcanoes National Park

The crown jewel of Rwanda and one of the only places on Earth where travelers can see **mountain gorillas** in the wild.

Why it's world-famous:

- Home of Dian Fossey's gorilla research
- Lush mountain rainforest
- Gorilla trekking (the top attraction in the country)
- Golden monkey trekking
- Stunning volcano views

A true bucket-list experience that many travelers describe as "life-changing."

2. Kigali (Africa's Cleanest Capital)

Kigali is modern, organized, green, and extremely safe — one of Africa's most impressive capitals.

Top attractions:

- Kigali Genocide Memorial
- Nyamirambo Women's Center
- Kimironko Market

- Art galleries & craft shops
- Coffee culture and modern restaurants
- Clean streets and beautiful viewpoints

Kigali is the perfect starting point for any Rwanda journey.

3. Nyungwe Forest National Park

A magical mountain rainforest filled with wildlife and ancient trees.

Highlights:

- **Chimpanzee trekking**
- **Canopy walkway** — one of Africa's most famous
- Hiking trails through dense green forest
- Birdwatching paradise (300+ species)
- Waterfall hikes

This park is ideal for nature lovers and adventure travelers.

4. Lake Kivu

A peaceful, relaxing lake shared between Rwanda and DR Congo — calm, warm, and perfect for resting after gorilla trekking.

Best towns:

- **Gisenyi (Rubavu)** — beaches, resorts, cafes
- **Kibuye (Karongi)** — beautiful views, boat rides
- **Cyangugu (Rusizi)** — quiet and scenic

Great for swimming, kayaking, sunset cruises, and relaxing.

Culture, Cleanliness & Safety

Rwanda is one of the **cleanest countries in the world** and the safest in East Africa. Travelers are always impressed by:

Cleanliness

- Monthly *Umuganda* community cleaning day
- No plastic bags allowed
- Clean public spaces, roads, and markets
- Beautiful gardens and green spaces everywhere

Safety

- Very low crime rate
- Friendly and respectful locals
- Strict but fair laws
- Excellent tourism infrastructure

Culture

Rwandans are known for their unity and resilience.

Cultural highlights:

- Traditional dances like *Intore*
- Beautiful woven baskets (*Agaseke*)
- Delicious dishes such as isombe, brochettes, and plantains
- Coffee and tea plantations
- Community tourism experiences in villages

Rwanda is welcoming, peaceful, and proud of its heritage.

How to Do Gorilla Trekking in Rwanda (2026 Guide)

Rwanda offers one of the world's best and most luxurious gorilla trekking experiences.

Permit Price (2026):

- $1,500 USD per person

What the permit includes:

- Park entry
- Trained rangers and guides

- Gorilla family allocation
- Safety briefings

Best trekking months:

- June–September
- December–February

Trek difficulty:

Moderate, depending on gorilla movement (2–6 hours).

What to bring:

- Hiking boots
- Rain jacket
- Long trousers
- Gloves (for forest vegetation)
- Packed water and snacks

Trekkers spend **one magical hour** with a gorilla family — a moment travelers never forget.

5-Day Rwanda Itinerary

Day 1 — Kigali

City tour, markets, local food.

Day 2 — Kigali Genocide Memorial + Drive to Musanze

Visit cultural sites, then travel to Volcanoes National Park.

Day 3 — Gorilla Trekking in Volcanoes National Park

An unforgettable wildlife experience.

Day 4 — Lake Kivu (Gisenyi)

Relax, swim, boat rides, coffee tours.

Day 5 — Return to Kigali → Departure

Shopping, art galleries, museums.

A quick but powerful introduction to Rwanda.

7-Day Rwanda Ultimate Itinerary

Day 1 — Arrive in Kigali

City exploration and dinner.

Day 2 — Kigali Cultural Tour

Markets, art, coffee, history.

Day 3 — Drive to Volcanoes National Park

Visit local villages and viewpoints.

Day 4 — Gorilla Trekking

Meet the mountain gorillas face-to-face.

Day 5 — Drive to Nyungwe Forest

Scenic mountain views.

Day 6 — Chimpanzee Trekking + Canopy Walk

Adventure in the rainforest.

Day 7 — Lake Kivu → Kigali → Departure

Relaxation and lakeside activities.

A perfect mix of culture, wildlife, and relaxation.

CHAPTER 8 — Multi-Country Itineraries

Exploring multiple East African countries in one trip is one of the most rewarding ways to experience the region. These itineraries are designed to help travelers maximize wildlife sightings, culture, beaches, and adventure — all in one unforgettable journey.

Kenya + Tanzania Safari (7–10 Days)

Perfect for: Big 5 safaris, Great Migration, adventure lovers.

Suggested Route

Nairobi → Maasai Mara → Serengeti → Ngorongoro Crater → Tarangire → Arusha

Highlights

- Witness the **Great Migration** between Maasai Mara & Serengeti
- Explore the legendary **Ngorongoro Crater**
- Scenic game drives in **Tarangire National Park**
- Cultural visits with the **Maasai communities**
- Optional hot air balloon safari

Travel Tips

- Best time: **June–October** & **January–February**
- Use border crossing: **Isebania** for a seamless transfer

Kenya + Uganda (Gorilla Trekking) — 8 Days

Perfect for: Safari + primates + adventure.

Suggested Route

Nairobi → Maasai Mara → Entebbe → Bwindi Impenetrable Forest → Kampala

Highlights

- Classic savannah safari in **Maasai Mara**
- Gorilla trekking experience in **Bwindi**
- Cultural encounters in **Kampala**
- Explore **Lake Bunyonyi** (optional)

Travel Tips

- Gorilla permits in Uganda remain more affordable than many regions.
- Book permits **months in advance** for 2026 travel.

Tanzania + Zanzibar — 10 Days

Perfect for: Safari + beach lovers.

Suggested Route

Arusha → Serengeti → Ngorongoro → Zanzibar (Stone Town & Beaches)

Highlights

- Safari in **Serengeti** & **Ngorongoro Crater**
- Fly from Arusha to Zanzibar for easy travel
- Explore **Stone Town**
- Relax on beaches like **Nungwi**, **Paje**, **Kendwa**, and **Jambiani**

Travel Tips

- Ideal for honeymoons and family vacations
- Beach resorts often have discounts from April–June

14-Day East Africa Master Itinerary

Perfect for: Travelers who want an all-in-one experience.

Suggested Route

Nairobi → **Maasai Mara** → **Serengeti** → **Ngorongoro** → **Arusha** → **Zanzibar** → **Kigali**

Highlights

- Best of **Kenya** & **Tanzania** wildlife
- Relaxation and culture in **Zanzibar**
- End with Rwanda's clean, modern capital: **Kigali**
- Optional gorilla trekking in **Volcanoes National Park**

Travel Tips

- Book internal flights early (especially Arusha → Zanzibar → Kigali)
- Great option for first-time East Africa travelers

21-Day Grand East Africa Loop

Perfect for: Enthusiastic explorers with time to see everything.

Suggested Route

Nairobi → Maasai Mara → Serengeti → Ngorongoro → Arusha → Zanzibar → Dar es Salaam → Entebbe → Bwindi → Kigali → Lake Kivu

Highlights

- Classic wildlife safaris
- Beaches & culture in Zanzibar

- Gorilla trekking in **Uganda or Rwanda**
- Peaceful lakeside retreats in **Lake Kivu**
- The most complete East African experience

Travel Tips

- Consider an **East Africa Tourist Visa** (Kenya–Uganda–Rwanda)
- Travel light and prepare for different climates

CHAPTER 9 — Budgeting & Money-Saving Secrets

Traveling across East Africa in 2026 does **not** have to be expensive. With the right planning, travelers can enjoy world-class safaris, beaches, and cultural experiences on almost any budget. This chapter reveals the smartest ways to save money while still having an unforgettable trip.

Cheapest Safari Options (2026 Guide)

Safaris can be costly, but these options help travelers enjoy wildlife without overspending:

1. Group Joining Safaris

- Shared vehicles = shared cost
- Available in **Kenya, Tanzania, and Uganda**
- Perfect for solo travelers or budget travelers

2. Shoulder Season Travel

- Visit during **March–May** or **October–November**
- Prices drop for lodges, tours, and flights
- Wildlife viewing is still excellent

3. Visit Less Crowded Parks

- More affordable than famous parks

- Examples: **Lake Manyara, Tarangire, Nairobi National Park, Samburu, Mikumi, Queen Elizabeth**

   4. Choose National Park Entry Passes Wisely

Prices vary per park — budget travelers should compare before planning multiple days.

Budget-Friendly Beaches

Travelers can enjoy East African beaches without expensive resorts.

Best Affordable Beaches

- **Nungwi (Zanzibar):** Many budget guesthouses
- **Kendwa (Zanzibar):** Cheaper in April–June
- **Diani Beach (Kenya):** Wide range of low-cost hotels
- **Bagamoyo (Tanzania):** Cultural and budget-friendly
- **Watamu (Kenya):** Beautiful and cheaper than most islands

Tips

- Book hotels with breakfast included
- Choose smaller boutique hotels rather than big resorts

Avoiding Tourist Scams

East Africa is generally friendly, but travelers should stay aware.

Common Things to Avoid

- Fake "tour guides" near airports or bus stations
- Overpriced taxi rides — always ask for the price first
- Fake souvenir sellers claiming "limited stock"
- Wildlife tour operators promising impossible animal sightings

How to Stay Safe

- Use recommendations from licensed tour companies
- Pay with card or secure mobile money where possible

- Keep valuables secure while walking in busy areas

Transport Tips

Travelers can save a lot on transport by planning wisely.

Best Budget Choices

- **Public buses** for long distances (Kenya–Uganda or Tanzania routes)
- **Domestic flight deals** between Nairobi, Arusha, Kilimanjaro & Zanzibar
- **Ride-hailing apps** like Uber/Bolt in major cities
- **Shared minibuses (matatus/dala-dalas)** for short routes (cheap but crowded)

Best Tip for 2026

Book flights early — demand will be high for the 2026 safari season.

When to Book for the Best Prices

Flights

- Book **3–6 months early** for the best deals

- Avoid peak periods: July–August & December

Safari Packages

- Best prices: **February–May**
- Lodges offer discounts before high season

Hotels

- Book early for Zanzibar (very high demand)
- Look for packages that include airport transfers

CHAPTER 10 — Accommodation Guide

East Africa offers a wide range of accommodations — from budget hostels and tented camps to world-class luxury lodges and beach resorts. This guide helps travelers choose the perfect places to stay in **Kenya, Tanzania, Zanzibar, Uganda, and Rwanda** based on their travel style and budget.

KENYA — Where Wildlife Meets Modern Comfort

Best Budget Options

- **Wildebeest Eco Camp (Nairobi)** — Affordable, nature-friendly stay
- **Diani Backpackers (Diani Beach)** — Social and perfect for beach lovers
- **Manyatta Camp (Tsavo)** — Budget-friendly tented camp near wildlife

Mid-Range Stays

- **Sarova Mara Game Camp (Maasai Mara)** — Classic safari comfort
- **Tamarind Tree Hotel (Nairobi)** — Clean, modern & well-located
- **The Sands at Nomad (Diani)** — Stylish rooms without luxury prices

Luxury Lodges

- **Angama Mara (Maasai Mara)** — Hilltop views & world-class service
- **Ol Tukai Lodge (Amboseli)** — Famous views of Kilimanjaro
- **Hemingways Nairobi** — Boutique luxury

Tented Camps

- **Basecamp Explorer (Maasai Mara)** — Nature-focused & eco-friendly
- **Porini Amboseli Camp** — Intimate wild experience

City Hotels

- **Radisson Blu (Nairobi)**
- **Eka Hotel (Nairobi)**

Beach Resorts

- Leopard Beach Resort (Diani)
- Baobab Beach Resort (Diani)

TANZANIA — Home of Serengeti & Kilimanjaro

Best Budget Options

- Nyumbani Hostel (Arusha)
- Kilimanjaro Backpackers (Moshi)
- Tarangire Simba Lodge (budget tents)

Mid-Range Stays

- Marera Valley Lodge (Karatu)
- Serengeti Heritage Camp
- Mount Meru Hotel (Arusha)

Luxury Lodges

- Four Seasons Safari Lodge (Serengeti)
- Ngorongoro Serena Safari Lodge
- Tarangire Treetops Lodge

Tented Camps

- **Kati Kati Tented Camp (Serengeti)**
- **Mapito Tented Camp**

City Hotels

- **Gran Melia Arusha**
- **Kibo Palace Hotel (Arusha)**

Beach Resorts (Mainland Tanzania)

- **Hyatt Regency Dar es Salaam**
- **Mediterraneo Hotel (Dar es Salaam)**

ZANZIBAR — Island Paradise

Best Budget Options

- **Lost & Found Hostel (Stone Town)**
- **Sagando Hostel (Michamvi)**
- **Makofi Guesthouse (Nungwi)**

Mid-Range Stays

- Mnarani Beach Cottages (Nungwi)
- Z Hotel (Nungwi)
- Casa Beach Hotel (Jambiani)

Luxury Resorts

- The Residence Zanzibar
- Park Hyatt Zanzibar (Stone Town)
- Gold Zanzibar Beach House & Spa (Kendwa)

Tented & Eco Beach Stays

- Chumbe Island Eco-Lodge
- Mnemba Island (exclusive private island)

City Hotels (Stone Town)

- Tembo House Hotel
- DoubleTree by Hilton Stone Town

UGANDA — Adventure, Rivers & Gorillas

Best Budget Options

- Backpackers Hostel (Kampala)
- Nile River Camp (Jinja)
- Lake Bunyonyi Overland Resort

Mid-Range Stays

- Fort Murchison Lodge
- Kyaninga Lodge
- Safari Lodge Bunyonyi

Luxury Lodges

- Bwindi Lodge (Bwindi)
- Paraa Safari Lodge (Murchison Falls)
- Chobe Safari Lodge

Tented Camps

- Bush Lodge (Queen Elizabeth NP)
- Haven Eco Camp (Jinja)

City Hotels

- Protea Hotel Kampala
- Serena Hotel Kampala

RWANDA — Safe, Clean & Scenic

Best Budget Options

- Mamba Village Hostel (Kigali)
- Discover Rwanda Youth Hostel

Mid-Range Stays

- Five to Five Hotel (Kigali)
- Lake Kivu Serena (Gisenyi)
- Nyungwe Top View Hill Hotel

Luxury Lodges

- Bisate Lodge (Volcanoes NP) — One of Africa's best lodges
- One&Only Nyungwe House
- The Retreat Kigali

City Hotels

- **Hotel des Mille Collines**
- **Kigali Marriott Hotel**

CHAPTER 11 — Packing List for 2026

Packing for East Africa in 2026 requires thoughtful preparation to enjoy **safaris, beaches, cultural tours, and adventure activities** comfortably. This chapter provides a complete list of essential items for a seamless trip.

Safari Clothes

Key Tips

- Lightweight, breathable, and neutral-colored clothing
- Avoid bright colors that may scare wildlife
- Layering is important — mornings and evenings can be cool

Essentials

- Long-sleeved shirts and trousers for sun and insect protection
- Shorts and t-shirts for warmer daytime
- Light jacket or fleece for early morning safaris
- Safari hat or cap
- Comfortable walking shoes or hiking boots

- Socks, underwear, and swimwear for lodges with pools

Beach Essentials

- Swimsuits and cover-ups
- Flip-flops or sandals
- Light summer dresses or shorts
- Beach towel and sarong
- Sunhat and sunglasses
- Reef-safe sunscreen (SPF 30+)
- Snorkeling gear (optional; can rent locally)
- Waterproof bag for electronics

Drone Rules (2026 Updates)

- Drone use is **strictly regulated** in many parks (Kenya, Tanzania, Uganda, Rwanda, Zanzibar)
- Must obtain **special permits** in national parks
- Avoid flying near wildlife, crowds, airports, or government buildings
- Check **local aviation authority regulations** before flying
- Always prioritize **safety and privacy**

Gadgets & Electronics

- Camera with extra batteries and memory cards
- Binoculars for safaris
- Smartphone and charger
- Power bank
- Universal travel adapter (East Africa uses types D, G, and M plugs)
- Optional: laptop or tablet

Travel Health Kit

- Prescription medications and copies of prescriptions
- Pain relievers, antihistamines, anti-diarrheal medication
- Insect repellent (DEET recommended)
- Hand sanitizer and wet wipes
- First aid kit: plasters, antiseptic wipes, bandages
- Water purification tablets or portable filter
- Sunscreen and lip balm with SPF
- Face masks and travel hygiene items

Extra Tips for 2026 Travelers

- Pack light: Internal flights often have strict luggage limits
- Use packing cubes for organized luggage
- Bring a daypack for safaris and city tours
- Leave valuables locked in hotel safes when not in use
- Keep travel documents, tickets, and permits in a waterproof pouch

CHAPTER 12 — Cultural Respect & Local Customs

Traveling isn't just about seeing new places—it's about connecting with people and respecting their way of life. Understanding local customs can turn an ordinary trip into a deeply enriching experience. This chapter guides you on how to immerse yourself respectfully and warmly.

1. Respectful Greetings

- A simple **"hello"** or **"good morning"** in the local language can go a long way.
- Observe local gestures: in some cultures, a handshake is formal; in others, a slight bow or nod is preferred.
- Avoid overly familiar gestures with strangers; modesty is often appreciated.

2. What NOT to Do

- Avoid pointing with fingers, raising your voice, or showing impatience.
- Steer clear of controversial topics like politics, religion, or local conflicts unless you are invited to discuss.

- Don't touch people's heads or personal belongings—this can be offensive in many cultures.

3. Dress Codes

- Some religious or rural areas have strict dress codes—covering shoulders, knees, and sometimes hair is expected.
- Swimwear is generally restricted to beaches and pools.
- Dressing modestly often earns respect and reduces unwanted attention.

4. Tipping Etiquette

- Learn the local tipping norms: in some countries it's expected, in others it may be unnecessary or even considered rude.
- Small gestures of appreciation, such as rounding up a bill or tipping 5–10%, often make a positive impression.
- Always carry small bills for convenience.

5. Photography Etiquette

- Always **ask before taking photos** of people, religious sites, or ceremonies.
- Avoid using flash in sensitive areas, like museums or temples.

- Respect signs that prohibit photography; following them shows cultural awareness.

6. How to Connect Warmly with Locals

- **Smile and make eye contact**—this is universally welcoming.
- Learn a few **local phrases** like "thank you" or "please."
- Participate respectfully in local traditions or festivals if invited.
- Show curiosity without being intrusive; locals often appreciate genuine interest in their culture.

Following these simple but crucial rules ensures your travels are **respectful, enriching, and memorable**. Not only will you avoid misunderstandings, but you'll also create authentic connections that make your journey unforgettable.

CHAPTER 13 — Hidden Gems Across East Africa

Beyond the famous safaris, beaches, and cities, East Africa is packed with secret spots that few travelers ever discover. Exploring these hidden gems gives you a more authentic, magical, and unforgettable experience. This chapter unveils the best secret places to explore, taste, and connect with local culture.

1. Secret Waterfalls

- **Hidden waterfalls** tucked away in lush forests or along remote hiking trails are perfect for adventure seekers.
- Swim in secluded pools and enjoy peaceful surroundings far from crowds.
- Ask local guides for insider directions, as many waterfalls aren't marked on maps.

2. Undiscovered Islands

- East Africa's coastline and lakes hold **undiscovered islands** with pristine beaches and untouched nature.
- Perfect for snorkeling, sunbathing, or simply relaxing in seclusion.

- Some islands are only accessible by small boats, adding to the sense of adventure.

3. Local Food Markets

- Explore bustling **local markets** for a true taste of East Africa.
- Sample fresh fruits, traditional snacks, spices, and street foods not found in tourist areas.
- Engage with friendly vendors—learning local food customs and recipes makes your experience richer.

4. Cultural Villages

- Visit **authentic villages** to experience traditional music, dance, crafts, and everyday life.
- Participate in workshops or guided tours to understand local customs respectfully.
- These visits create meaningful connections and support local communities directly.

5. Off-the-Path Safari Camps

- While famous parks like Serengeti and Maasai Mara draw crowds, **remote safari camps** offer exclusive wildlife encounters.

- Enjoy personalized game drives, private lodges, and intimate encounters with nature.
- Many of these hidden camps support conservation efforts and offer eco-friendly stays.

Discovering these **hidden gems** transforms a standard trip into a journey of wonder, adventure, and cultural immersion. By stepping off the beaten path, you'll uncover **the East Africa few travelers ever see**, creating memories that last a lifetime.

CHAPTER 14— Safety, Transport & Practical Tips

Traveling across East Africa is thrilling, but staying safe and navigating efficiently ensures your trip is smooth, enjoyable, and stress-free. This chapter provides essential guidance on safety, transportation, and practical updates for 2026.

1. Safety Do's and Don'ts

- **Do:**
    - Keep valuables secure and carry copies of important documents.
    - Use registered guides and tour operators, especially for safaris and adventure activities.
    - Stay informed about local conditions via news, apps, or hotel staff.
- **Don't:**
    - Walk alone at night in unfamiliar areas.
    - Ignore wildlife rules—maintain safe distances in parks.
    - Flaunt expensive gadgets or large amounts of cash.

2. Best Local Airlines

- Regional flights save time between countries and major destinations. Recommended carriers include:
    - **Kenya Airways** (Kenya)
    - **Ethiopian Airlines** (Ethiopia & regional hubs)
    - **RwandAir** (Rwanda)
    - **Precision Air** (Tanzania)
    - **Airlink** (Zanzibar & smaller islands)
- Booking early often gets the best fares, and some airlines offer flexible tickets for safari travelers.

3. Bus / Boat / Train Options

- **Buses:** Affordable and reliable for local and intercity travel. Look for reputable companies with air-conditioned coaches.
- **Boats:** Essential for islands, lakes, and coastal villages. Safety varies, so check boat conditions and life jackets.
- **Trains:** Limited but scenic routes, such as Kenya's Madaraka Express. Ideal for travelers who enjoy views and comfort over speed.

4. Border Crossing Rules

- East African countries have different visa requirements; check current regulations for 2026.
- **EAC (East African Community) visa** allows entry into Kenya, Uganda, and Rwanda with a single permit.
- Always carry passport copies, vaccination certificates (especially yellow fever), and proof of onward travel.
- Be prepared for customs checks—declare electronics, cash, or restricted items as required.

5. 2026 Updates

- Safety guidelines may change based on local advisories; check official tourism boards before departure.
- Some new ferry routes and low-cost airlines are emerging, offering cheaper and faster transport options.
- Mobile payment and digital ticketing systems are increasingly used for buses, trains, and ferries—download relevant apps.
- Keep an eye on new eco-friendly lodges, camps, and sustainable tourism initiatives across East Africa.

Following these **practical tips** ensures that your East Africa journey is safe, efficient, and enjoyable. With the right planning, transport knowledge, and safety awareness, you can focus on **adventure, discovery, and unforgettable experiences**.

Printed in Dunstable, United Kingdom